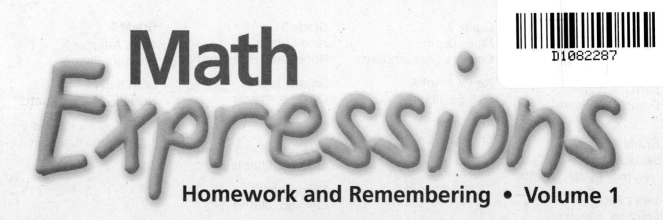

Math Expressions

Homework and Remembering • Volume 1

Developed by
The Children's Math Worlds Research Project

PROJECT DIRECTOR AND AUTHOR
Dr. Karen C. Fuson

This material is based upon work supported by the
National Science Foundation
under Grant Numbers
ESI-9816320, REC-9806020, and RED-935373.

Any opinions, findings, and conclusions, or recommendations expressed in this material
are those of the author and do not necessarily reflect the views of the National Science Foundation.

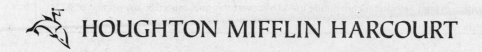

HOUGHTON MIFFLIN HARCOURT

Teacher Reviewers

Kindergarten
Patricia Stroh Sugiyama
Wilmette, Illinois

Barbara Wahle
Evanston, Illinois

Grade 1
Sandra Budson
Newton, Massachusetts

Janet Pecci
Chicago, Illinois

Megan Rees
Chicago, Illinois

Grade 2
Molly Dunn
Danvers, Massachusetts

Agnes Lesnick
Hillside, Illinois

Rita Soto
Chicago, Illinois

Grade 3
Jane Curran
Honesdale, Pennsylvania

Sandra Tucker
Chicago, Illinois

Grade 4
Sara Stoneberg Llibre
Chicago, Illinois

Sheri Roedel
Chicago, Illinois

Grade 5
Todd Atler
Chicago, Illinois

Leah Barry
Norfolk, Massachusetts

Special Thanks

Special thanks to the many teachers, students, parents, principals, writers, researchers, and work-study students who participated in the Children's Math Worlds Research Project over the years.

Credits

(t) © G. K. Hart/Vikki Hart/Getty Images, (b) Photodisc/Getty Images.

Illustrative art: Ginna Magee and Burgandy Beam/Wilkinson Studio; Tim Johnson
Technical art: Anthology, Inc.

ISBN: 978-0-547-06666-0

12 13 14 0982 17 16 15 14 13
4500406647

ii

Homework

Draw 5 trees.	Draw 3 bees.

Draw 4 rocks.	Draw 2 socks.

On the Back Draw 3 people. Then practice writing the numbers 1 and 2.

Count From 1 to 10 1

Homework

Name _____

Ring the pictures that are the same/alike.

Cross out the picture that is different/not alike.

1.

6.

2.

7.

3.

8.

4.

9.

5.

10.

➜ **On the Back** Draw 2 birds that are the same size and I bird that is a different size.

Then practice writing the number 3.

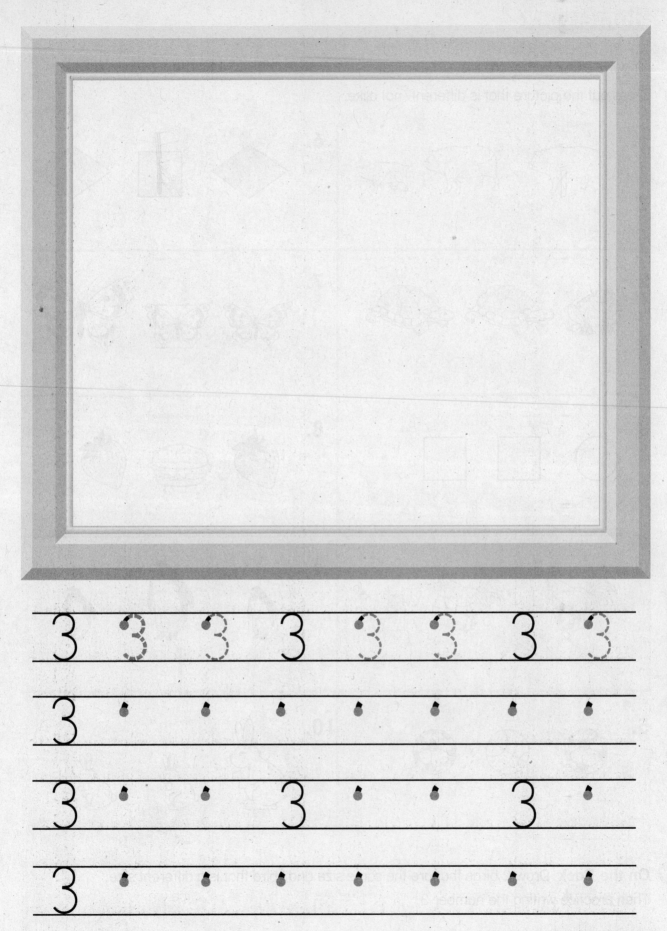

Exploration of Shapes

Practice

Ring the pictures that are the same/alike.

Cross out the picture that is different/not alike.

1.

6.

2.

7.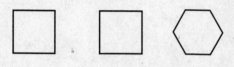

3.

8.

4.

9.

5.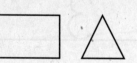

10.

On the Back Draw a picture of 3 things that are different. Then practice writing the number 3.

Name

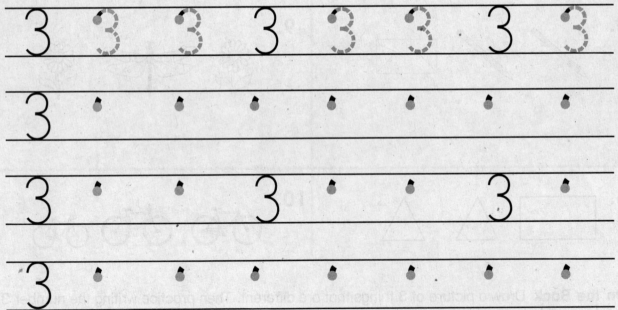

3 3 3 3 3 3 3 3

3

3 3 3

3 3 3

Objects and Numbers Through 10: Square-Inch Tiles

Homework

Draw 2 dogs.	Draw 4 logs.
Draw 3 bugs.	Draw 5 mugs.

On the Back Draw 5 animals. Then practice writing the numbers 1 and 2.

Number of Objects in a Group

Name _____

Practice

Go left to right. Ring groups of the number. X out groups that are not the number.

3

4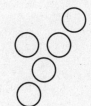

5

2

➡ **On the Back** Draw a group of 5 squares. Then practice writing the number 3.

2- and 3-Dimensional Shapes: Circle and Ball **9**

Name _____

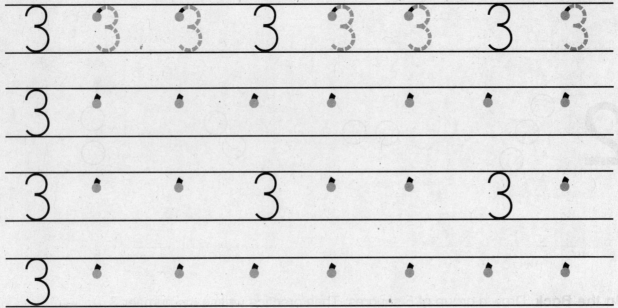

2- and 3-Dimensional Shapes: Circle and Ball

Name _____

Homework

Draw 5 eggs.	Draw 2 legs.
Draw 4 boats.	Draw 3 coats.

⬤➤ **On the Back** Draw 2 goats. Then practice writing the number 4.

More Numbers of Objects in a Group

Name _____

Practice

Go left to right. Ring groups of the number. X out groups that are not the number.

3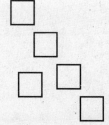

4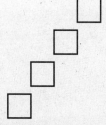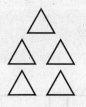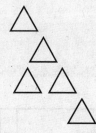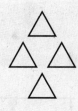

5

2

⮕ **On the Back** Draw 4 triangles. Then practice writing the number 4.

Objects and Numbers Through 10: Centimeter Cubes **13**

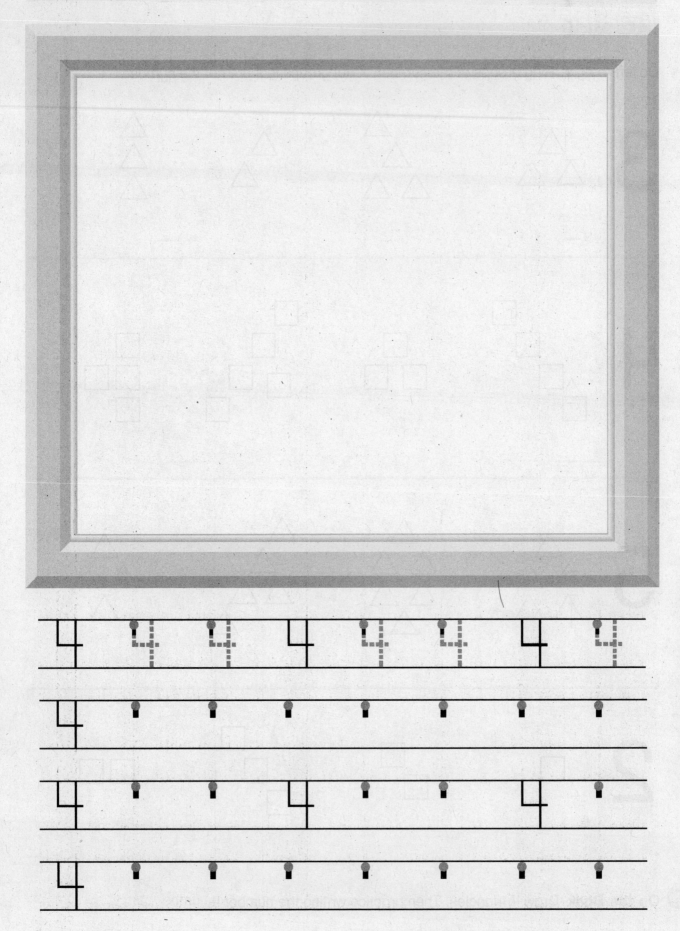

Objects and Numbers Through 10: Centimeter Cubes

Homework

Go left to right. Ring groups of the number. X out groups that are not the number.

3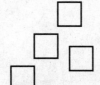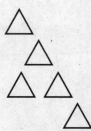

4

5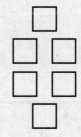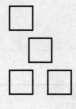

2

🔘 **On the Back** Draw a group of 5 cherries. Then practice writing the number 5.

5 5 5 5 5 5 5

5

5 5 5

5

Practice: Number of Objects in a Group

Homework

Connect the dots in order.

• 1   • 3

• 2

• 2   • 4

• 1   • 3

• 2   • 1

• 3   • 4

• 1   • 3   • 5

• 2   • 4

On the Back Practice drawing straight lines. Draw lines that go up and down. Also draw lines that go from left to right.

More Objects and Numbers Through 10: Square-Inch Tiles

Name _____

Homework

Go left to right. Ring groups of the number. X out groups that are not the number.

3

4

5

2

⮕ **On the Back** Draw a group of 2 and a group of 4. Then practice writing the number 5.

Name _____

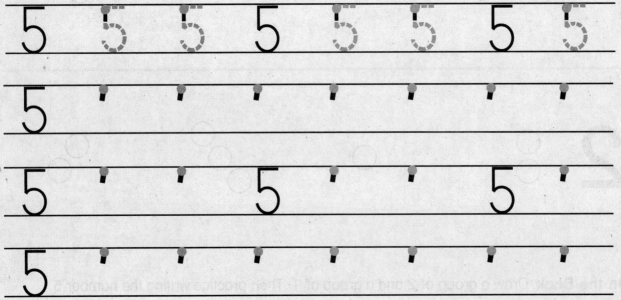

More Scenes of 2, 3, 4, and 5

Practice

1. Draw 5 bugs.

2. Draw 2 rugs.

3. Draw 4 trucks.

4. Draw 3 ducks.

On the Back Practice writing the numbers 1, 2, 3, 4, and 5.

More Objects and Numbers Through 10: Centimeter Cubes **21**

1 1 1 1 1 1 1

1

2 2 2 2 2 2 2 2

2

3 3 3 3 3 3 3 3

3

4 4 4 4 4 4 4 4

4

5 5 5 5 5 5 5 5

5

More Objects and Numbers Through 10: Centimeter Cubes

Homework

Name

Go left to right. Ring groups of the number. X out groups that are not the number.

3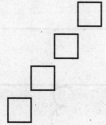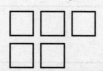

4

5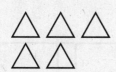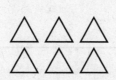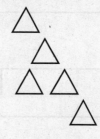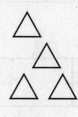

2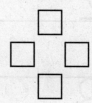

On the Back Practice writing the numbers 1, 2, 3, 4, and 5.

1

1

2 2 2 2 2 2 2 2

2

3 3 3 3 3 3 3 3

4 4 4 4 4 4 4 4

4

5 5 5 5 5 5 5 5

5

Scenes of I

Name _____

Practice

Connect the dots in order.

⬤ **On the Back** Draw your own dot-to-dot picture.

Make a Class Graph

Name _____

Homework

Look at this group of shapes.

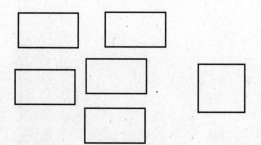

Circle a shape if it belongs in the group.

Cross out a shape if it does not belong in the group.

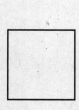

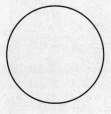

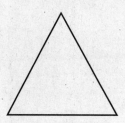

On the Back Draw 2 shapes that belong in the group.

Use Mathematical Processes

Name _____

Homework

Go left to right. Ring groups of the number. X out groups that are not the number.

2

5

4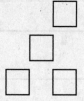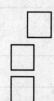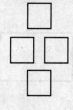

3

➡ **On the Back** Draw a group of 6. Then practice writing the numbers 1, 2, 3, 4, and 5.

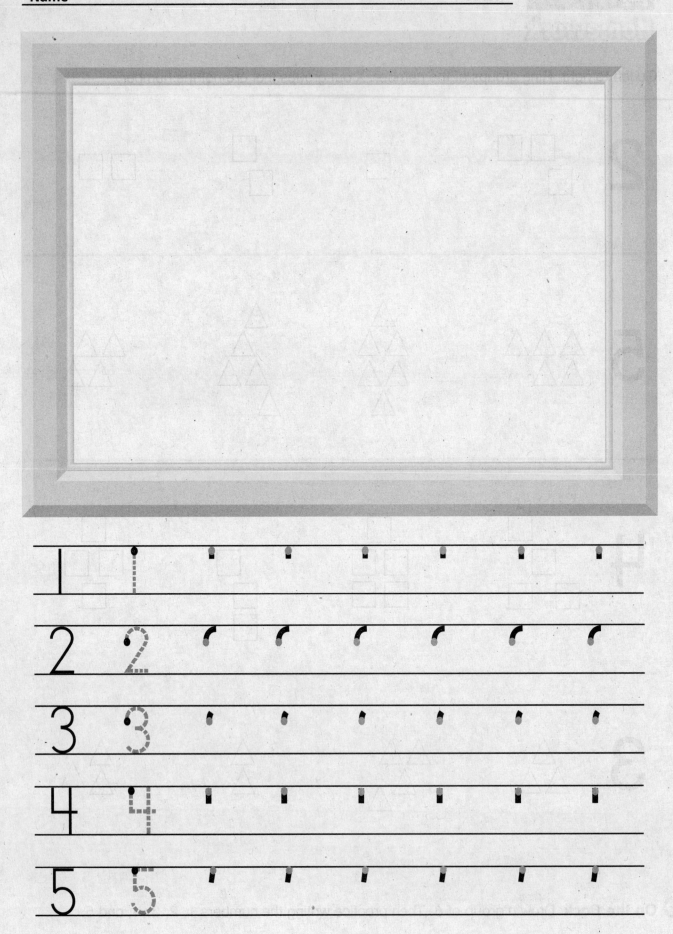

1

2

3

4

5

Relate Objects and Numbers 6–10

Name _____

Ring groups of the number. X out groups that are not the number.

6

7

8

9

10

 On the Back Draw a group of 8. Then practice writing the numbers 1, 2, 3, 4, and 5.

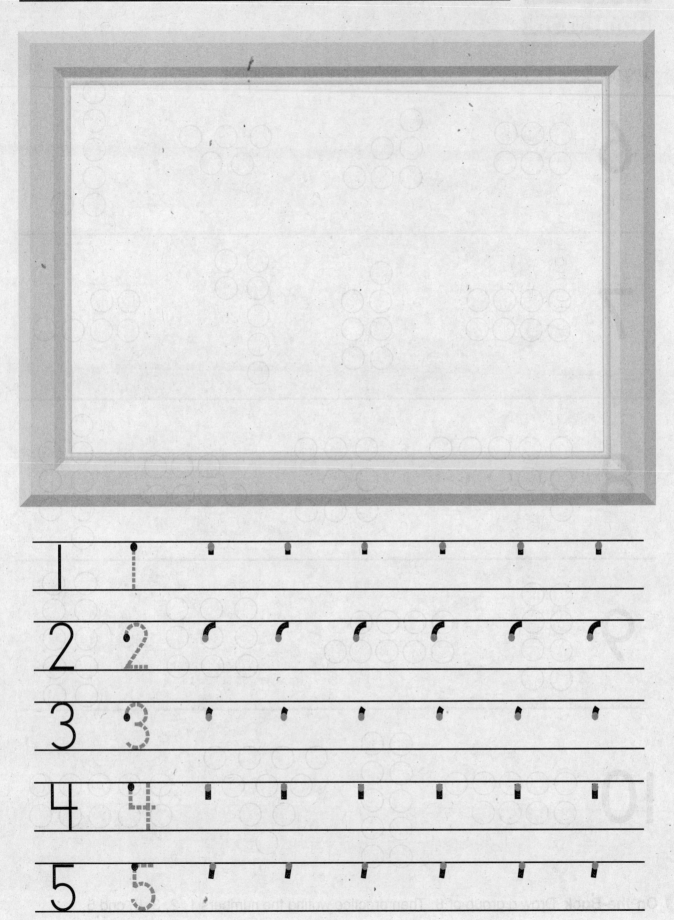

1
2
3
4
5

Family Math Stories

Homework

Ring groups of the number. X out groups that are not the number.

6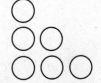

7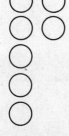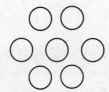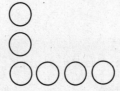

8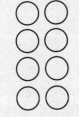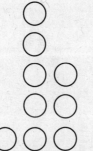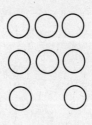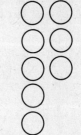

9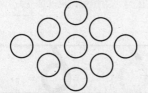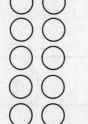

10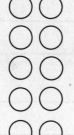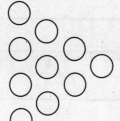

On the Back Draw a group of 6. Then practice writing the number 6.

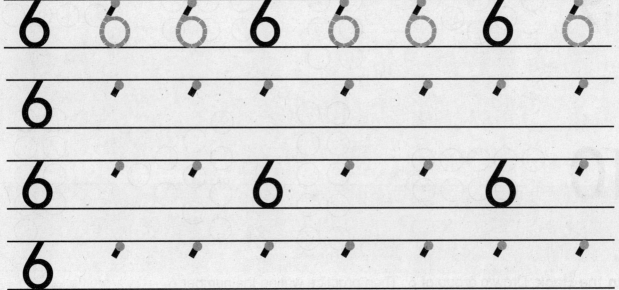

More Family Math Stories

Name

Homework

Ring groups of the number. X out groups that are not the number.

6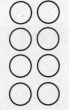

7

8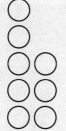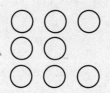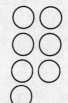

9

10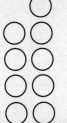

⟡ **On the Back** Draw 8 circles. Use a 5-group.

Make Repeating Patterns

Practice

Continue the pattern.

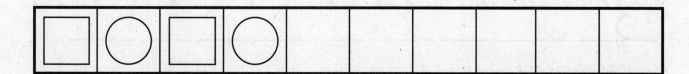

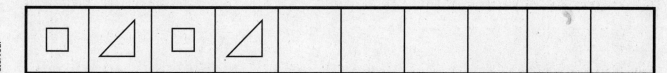

Draw your own patterns.

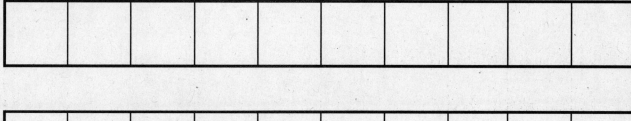

🡢 **On the Back** Practice writing the numbers 1–6.

1   1

2   2

3   3

4   4

5   5

6   6

Homework

Connect the dots in order.

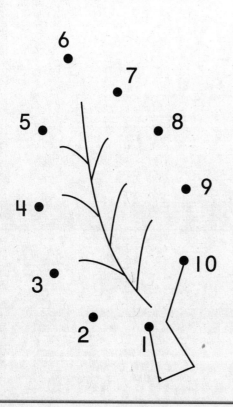

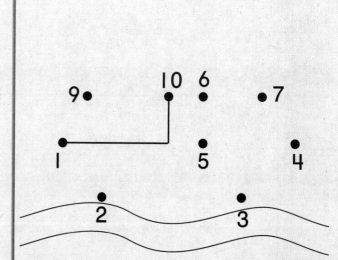

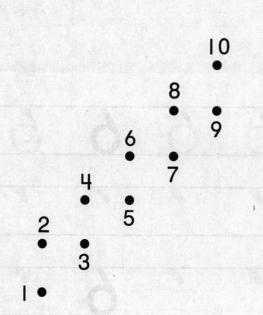

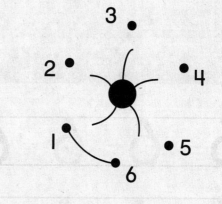

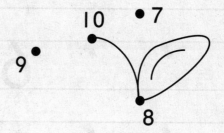

On the Back Draw 6 flowers. Then practice writing the number 6.

6 6 6 6 6 6 6 6

6

6 6 6

6

More Coin Values and Numbers 6–10

Name _____

Practice

Ring groups of the number. X out groups that are not the number.

6

7

8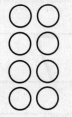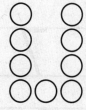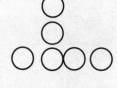

9

10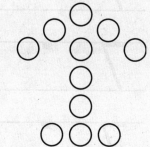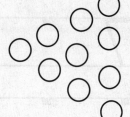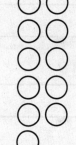

🡆 **On the Back** Draw a group of 7 rectangles. Then practice writing the number 7.

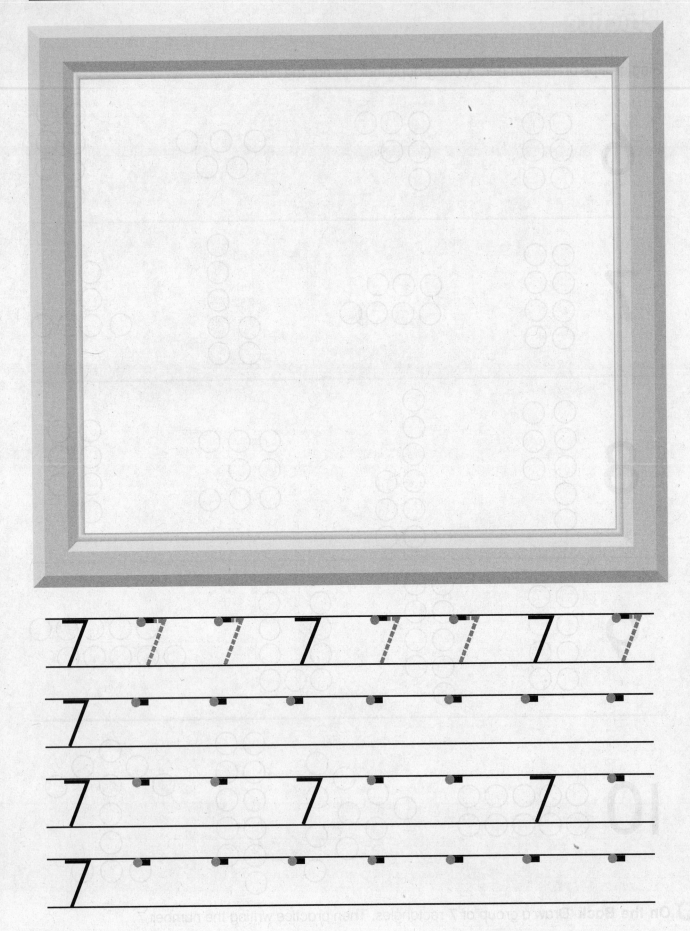

2- and 3-Dimensional Shapes: Rectangles and Boxes

Name _____

Homework

Draw shapes in each box to show that number.

1	2
3	**4**
5	

➡ **On the Back** Use shapes to draw patterns.

Practice with 5-Groups **43**

Practice with 5-Groups

Homework

Ring groups of the number. X out groups that are not the number.

6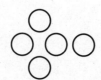

7

8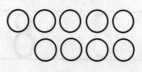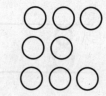

9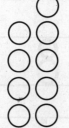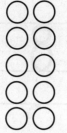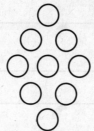

10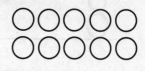

On the Back Draw 8 bugs. Then practice writing the number 8.

Explore Number Patterns **45**

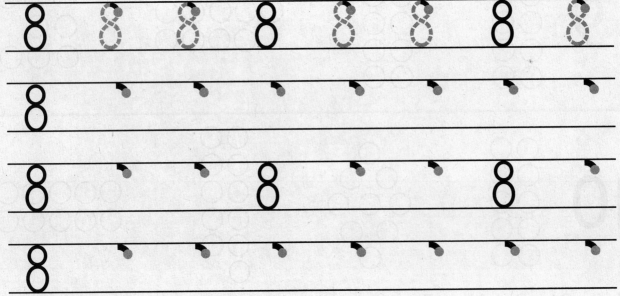

Explore Number Patterns

Name _____

Practice

Ring groups of the number. X out groups that are not the number.

6

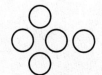 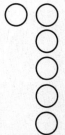

7

  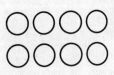 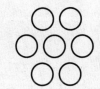

8

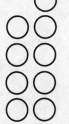 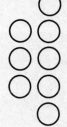 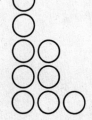

9

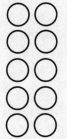  

10

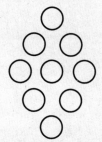

➡ **On the Back** Draw a group of 9 rectangles.

More Repeating Patterns **47**

More Repeating Patterns

Homework

Use a pencil or marker and trace
each number 2 times.

| 3 | ● ● ● |
| 5 | ● ● ● ● ● |

3 5
  3   3   5   3   5   3
5   5   3
    5   3   3   5   5
3   3   3
      5   3   3   3
   5   3   5   5
5   3   3   3
                 5

Write numbers 1–10.

➡ **On the Back** Draw 5 triangles. Write the number 5.

Name _____

Practice

Use a pencil or marker and trace
each number 2 times.

4	●●●●
6	●●●●● ●

6
4
6
6
4
4
6
4
6
4
6
4
6
4
6
4
6
4
6
4
6
6
4
4
6
4
6
4
6
4
6
4
6

Write numbers 1–8.

➡ **On the Back** Draw 9 carrots. Then practice writing the number 9.

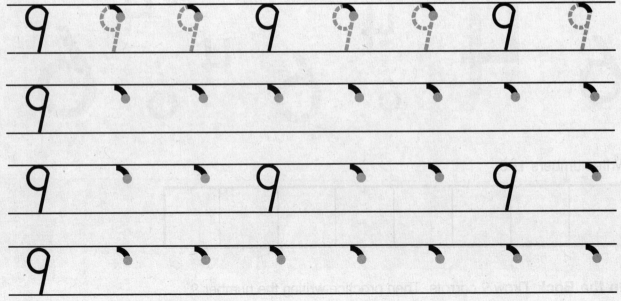

Addition and Subtraction Stories: Garden Scenario

Homework

Draw 6 hats.	Draw 9 mats.
Draw 7 cats.	Draw 8 bats.

On the Back Write the numbers 1–9 in all different sizes.

Numbers 1 Through 10: the +1 Pattern

Name _____

Homework

Continue the pattern.

| 2 | 5 | 2 | 5 | | | | | | |

| ○ | ▯ | ○ | ▯ | | | | | | |

| ▢ | ○ | ○ | ▢ | ○ | ○ | | | |

| △ | △ | △ | △ | △ | △ | | | |

| 3 | 3 | 5 | 3 | 3 | 5 | | | |

Draw your own patterns.

| | | | | | | | | | |

| | | | | | | | | | |

🔵 **On the Back** Draw your own patterns.

More Numbers 1 Through 10: the +1 Pattern **55**

Name _____

More Numbers 1 Through 10: the +1 Pattern

Name _____

Practice

Use a pencil or marker and trace
each number 2 times.

| 4 | ● ● ● ● |

| 8 | ● ● ● ● ● ● ● ● |

8

4

8

8

8

4

4

8

4

4

8

8

4

8

8

4

8

8

8

4

4

8

4

8

4

8

4

8

4

8

8

8

8

4

4

8

Write the numbers 1–10.

On the Back Draw a picture of 4 children playing.

Addition and Subtraction Stories: Family Experience **57**

Addition and Subtraction Stories: Family Experience

Homework

Draw 7 cars.	Draw 6 jars.

Draw 9 books.	Draw 8 hooks.

On the Back Draw a group of 10. Then practice writing the number 10.

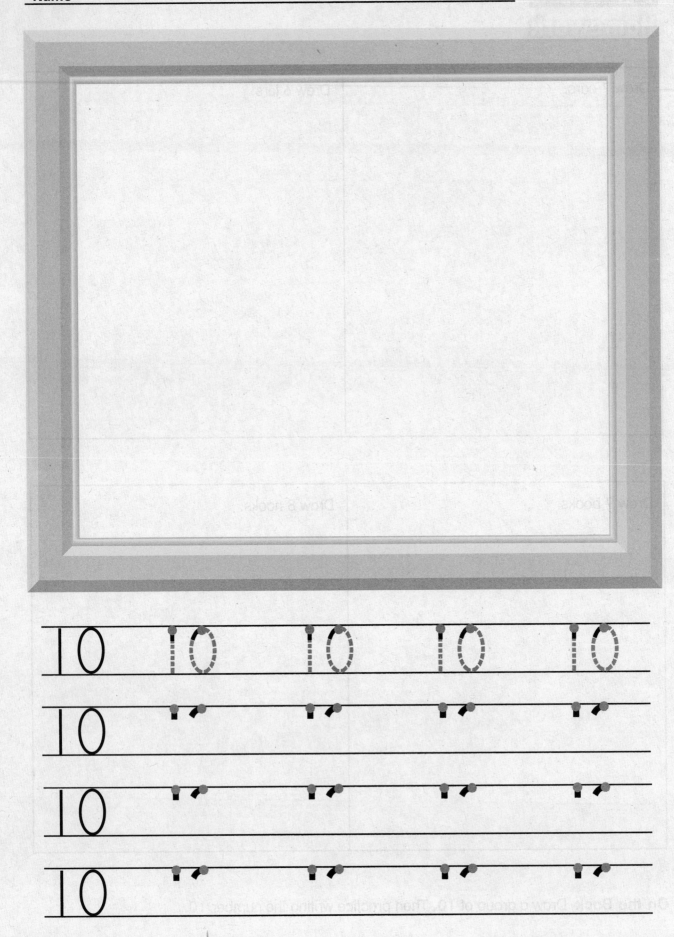

Numbers 1 Through 10: the –1 Pattern

Name _____

Practice

Use a pencil or marker and trace
each number 2 times.

5

9

Write the numbers 1–10.

On the Back Write the numbers 1–9 in all different sizes.

Name

Number Writing Practice

Homework

Write numbers 4 and 5.

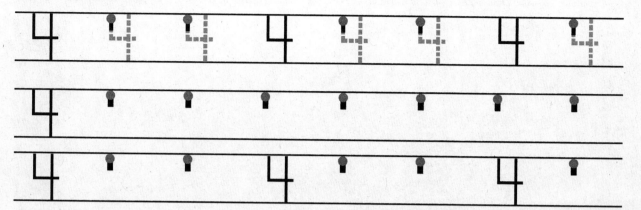

Draw 4 things.	Draw 4 rectangles.

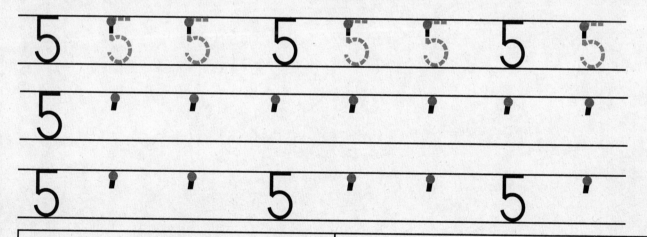

Draw 5 things.	Draw 5 squares.

 On the Back Draw 10 animals.

Homework

Use a pencil or marker. Trace all the
numbers 2 times.

| 3 | ● ● ● |
| 8 | ● ● ● ● ●
 ● ● ● |

8 8

3   8

3   3   3

8   3   3

8   8   8   3   8

8   8   3   3   8

3   3   3

3   3   8   3

3   8   3   8

8   3   8   8

Write numbers 1–10.

🔶 **On the Back** Write the number 8, and draw 8 trees.

Groups of 10

Homework

Name

Write the number.

1.

2.

3.

4.

5. Continue the pattern.

On the Back Draw your own patterns.

Addition and Subtraction Stories: Park Scene **67**

Addition and Subtraction Stories: Park Scene

Homework

1. Write the number pattern in each row.

●● 2	●●● 3	●●●● 4	●●●●● 5	●● 2	●●● 3	●●●● 4	●●●●● 5

2. Write the number.

3.

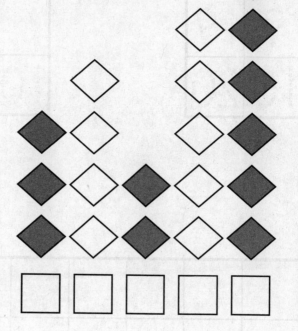

On the Back Write the numbers 1–20.

1	11
2	12
3	13
4	14
5	15
6	16
7	17
8	18
9	19
10	20

1	11
10	20

More Addition and Subtraction Stories: Park Scene

Name _____

Write the number.

1.

2.

3.

4.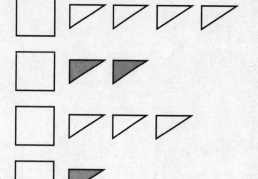

5. Write numbers 1–20.

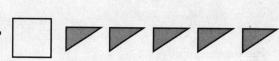

🔄 **On the Back** Use shapes to make a picture.

Use a Balance Scale to Graph Weight

Homework

1. Finish the 5-group that shows the same number.

 = ☐

○ ○ ○ ○ ○

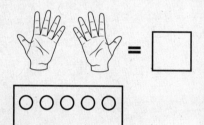 = ☐

○ ○ ○ ○ ○

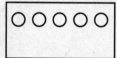 = ☐

○ ○ ○ ○ ○

🖐🖐 = ☐

○ ○ ○ ○ ○

2. Finish the 5-groups.

7 = | ○ ○ ○ ○ ○ |

9 = | ○ ○ ○ ○ ○ |

6 = | ○ ○ ○ ○ ○ |

8 = | ○ ○ ○ ○ ○ |

8 = | ○ ○ ○ ○ ○ |

10 = | ○ ○ ○ ○ ○ |

10 = | ○ ○ ○ ○ ○ |

6 = | ○ ○ ○ ○ ○ |

3. Write the number.

| ○ ○ ○ ○ ○ ○ ○ | = ☐ | ○ ○ ○ ○ ○ ○ ○ ○ ○ ○ | = ☐

| ○ ○ ○ ○ ○ ○ ○ | = ☐ | ○ ○ ○ | = ☐

| ○ ○ ○ ○ ○ ○ ○ | = ☐ | ○ ○ ○ ○ ○ ○ ○ ○ ○ | = ☐

| ○ ○ ○ ○ ○ ○ | = ☐ | ○ ○ ○ ○ ○ | = ☐

🔘 **On the Back** Draw different animals then write the numbers 1 to 20.

Name _____

Practice Addition and Subtraction Stories: Park Scene

Homework

1. Write the number pattern in each row.

••	•••••	••••• •••	••	•••••	••••• •••	••	•••••	••••• •••
2	5	8	2	5	8	2	5	8

2. Repeat the pattern.

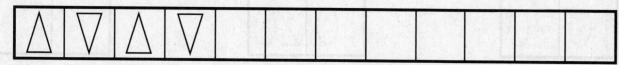

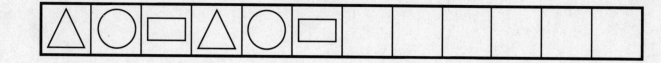

➡ **On the Back** Write the numbers 1–20.

1	11
2	12
3	13
4	14
5	15
6	16
7	17
8	18
9	19
10	20

11	11
10	20

More Attributes: Size, Shape, and Color

Practice

1. Continue the pattern.

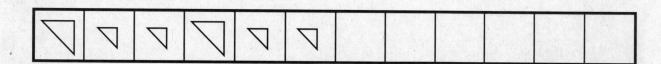

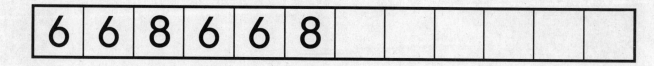

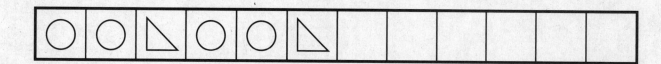

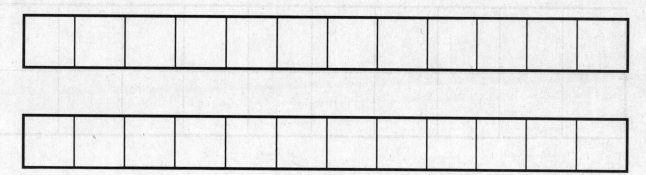

2. Draw your own patterns.

🡢 **On the Back** Draw 9 different flowers. Then write the numbers 1–20.

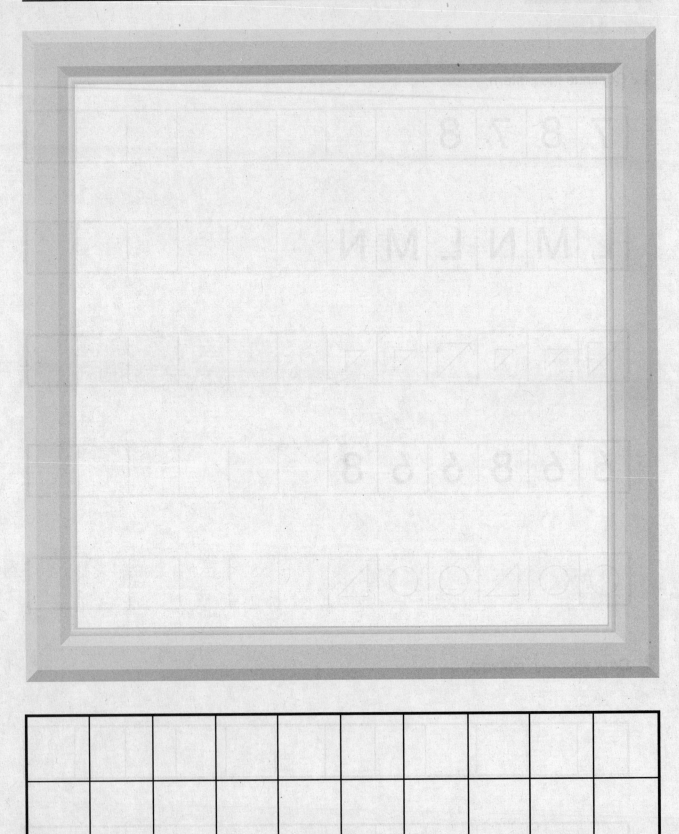

Build Teen Numbers with Square-Inch Tiles

Name _____

Homework

1. Draw circles for 1–10.
Show the 5-groups.

1	
2	
3	
4	
5	
6	
7	○ ○ ○ ○ ○ ○ ○
8	
9	
10	

2. Finish the 5-groups.

6 = ○ ○ ○ ○ ○   8 = ○ ○ ○ ○ ○

8 = ○ ○ ○ ○ ○   9 = ○ ○ ○ ○ ○

10 = ○ ○ ○ ○ ○   7 = ○ ○ ○ ○ ○

9 = ○ ○ ○ ○ ○   10 = ○ ○ ○ ○ ○

3. Write the number.

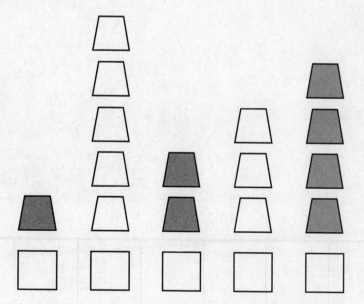

4. On the Back Draw 7 different houses. Then write the numbers 1–20.

Attribute Card Activities

Name _____

Practice

Write the number.

1.

2.

3.

4.

Finish the pattern.

5.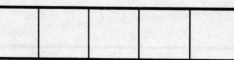

8	8	2	8	8	2					

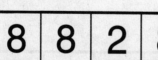 **On the Back** Draw your own patterns.

Tens in Teens **81**

Name

Tens in Teens

Homework

1. Write the number pattern in each row.

●●	●●●●	●●●●● ●●●	●●	●●●●	●●●●● ●●●	●●	●●●●	●●●●● ●●●
2	4	8	2	4	8	2	4	8

2. Repeat the pattern.

△	□	○	△	□	○						

▭	◺	▭	◺								

□	○	▯	□	○	▯						

➡ **On the Back** Draw your own patterns.

Graph Drawings: Match and Compare **83**

Name _____

Graph Drawings: Match and Compare

Name _____

Homework

1. Write the number pattern in each row.

4	6	9	4	6	9	4	6	9

2. Repeat the pattern.

🡆 **On the Back** Write the numbers 1–10 in all different sizes.

2- and 3-Dimensional Shapes: Squares and Cubes **85**

Name

2- and 3-Dimensional Shapes: Squares and Cubes

Name

Write the partners.

2

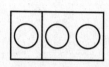

☐ + ☐

3

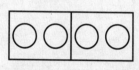

☐ + ☐

3

☐ + ☐

4

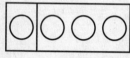

☐ + ☐

4

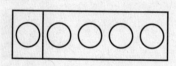

☐ + ☐

4

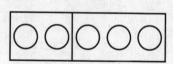

☐ + ☐

5

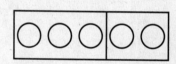

☐ + ☐

5

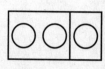

☐ + ☐

5

☐ + ☐

6

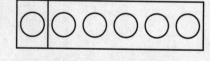

☐ + ☐

6

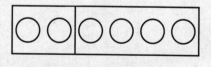

☐ + ☐

6

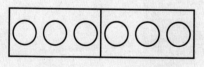

☐ + ☐

On the Back Draw a picture for 2 + 3 in the top box.

Draw a picture for 3 + 1 in the bottom box.

More Graph Drawings: Match and Compare **87**

More Graph Drawings: Match and Compare

Name _____

Practice

1. Write the number pattern in each row.

♦♦♦	♦♦♦♦	♦♦♦♦♦	♦♦♦	♦♦♦♦	♦♦♦♦♦	♦♦♦	♦♦♦♦	♦♦♦♦♦
3	4	5	3	4	5	3	4	5

2. Repeat the pattern.

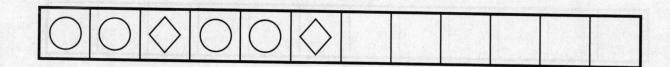

▽	△	▽	△							

○	○	◇	○	○	◇					

J	K	L	J	K	L					

🡆 **On the Back** Draw your own patterns.

More Teen Numbers with Classroom Objects

Homework

1. Draw circles for 1–10. Show the 5-groups.

1	
2	
3	
4	
5	
6	
7	
8	
9	○○○○○ ○○○○
10	

2. Write each number and = or ≠.

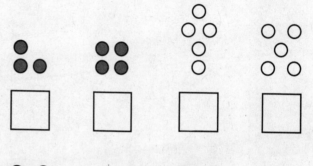

2 ≠ 4

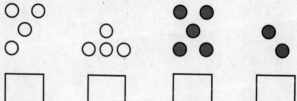

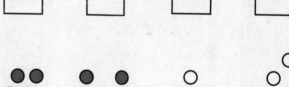

3. Finish the 5-groups.

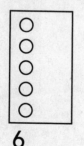
6

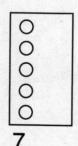
7

8

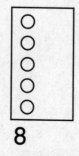
9

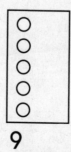
10

➡ **On the Back** Draw two groups of circles. Write = or ≠.

More Attribute Card Activities

Name _____

Practice

1. Finish the 5-group to show the number.

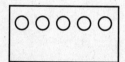
= ☐

○ ○ ○ ○ ○

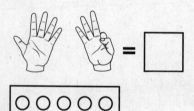
= ☐

○ ○ ○ ○ ○

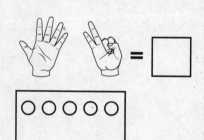
= ☐

○ ○ ○ ○ ○

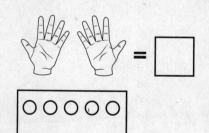
= ☐

○ ○ ○ ○ ○

2. Finish the 5-groups.

10 = ○ ○ ○ ○ ○   8 = ○ ○ ○ ○ ○

6 = ○ ○ ○ ○ ○   6 = ○ ○ ○ ○ ○

7 = ○ ○ ○ ○ ○   8 = ○ ○ ○ ○ ○

9 = ○ ○ ○ ○ ○   7 = ○ ○ ○ ○ ○

3. Write the number.

○ ○ ○ ○ ○ / ○ ○ ○ = ☐   ○ ○ = ☐

○ ○ ○ ○ ○ / ○ = ☐   ○ ○ ○ ○ ○ / ○ ○ = ☐

○ ○ ○ ○ ○ / ○ ○ = ☐   ○ ○ ○ ○ ○ / ○ = ☐

○ ○ ○ ○ ○ / ○ ○ ○ ○ = ☐   ○ ○ ○ ○ ○ = ☐

⬤ **On the Back** Use shapes to make a picture.

Object Collections: Teen Numbers

Homework

Name _____

1. Write the number pattern in each row.

✦✦✦	✦✦✦✦✦ ✦	✦✦✦✦✦ ✦✦✦✦	✦✦✦	✦✦✦✦✦ ✦	✦✦✦✦✦ ✦✦✦✦	✦✦✦	✦✦✦✦✦ ✦	✦✦✦✦✦ ✦✦✦✦
3	6	9	3	6	9	3	6	9

2. Write each number and = or ≠.

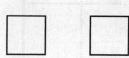

| 5 | = | 5 |

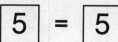

⟹ On the Back Write the numbers 1–20.

1	1
2	2
3	3
4	4
5	5
6	6
7	7
8	8
9	9
10	20

1	1
10	20

Shapes in a Garden Scene

Homework

1. Ring the answer for the number of circles.

8 + 2   5 + 3   5 + 8

2. Ring the answer for the number of squares.

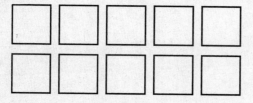

5 + 10   5 + 0   5 + 5

3. Ring the answer for the number of triangles.

5 + 1   6 + 4   6 + 1

4. Ring the drawing that shows how to share 8 marbles with 4 people.

On the Back Show how to share 15 marbles with 5 people.

Use Mathematical Processes **97**

Use Mathematical Processes